THE
ISLE OF WIGHT
A Pictorial History

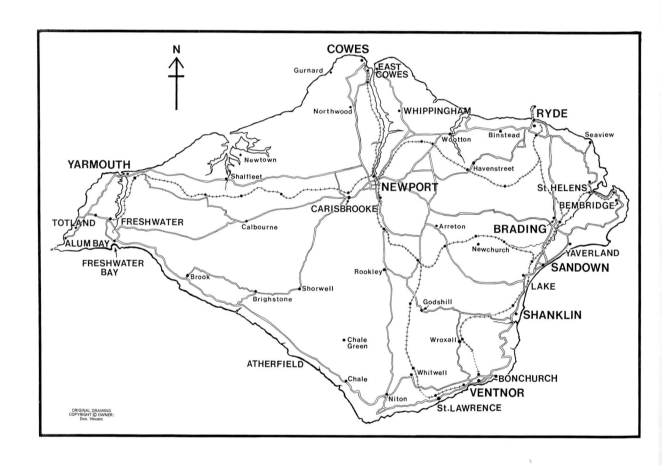

N

COWES

Gurnard

EAST
COWES

Northwood

WHIPPINGHAM

RYDE

Seaview

Binstead

Wootton

Newtown

Havenstreet

YARMOUTH

Shalfleet

St.HELENS

NEWPORT

BEMBRIDGE

TOTLAND

CARISBROOKE

FRESHWATER

BRADING

Calbourne

Arreton

ALUM BAY

YAVERLAND

Newchurch

FRESHWATER
BAY

Rookley

SANDOWN

Brook

Shorwell

LAKE

Brighstone

Godshill

SHANKLIN

Chale
Green

Wroxall

ATHERFIELD

Whitwell

BONCHURCH

Chale

VENTNOR

Niton

St.LAWRENCE

ORIGINAL DRAWING
COPYRIGHT © OWNER:
Don. Vincent

THE ISLE OF WIGHT

A Pictorial History

Sheila Caws

Phillimore

1989

Published by
PHILLIMORE & CO. LTD
Shopwyke Hall, Chichester, Sussex

ISBN 0 85033 691 0

Printed and bound in Great Britain by
BIDDLES LTD.
Guildford, Surrey

To Bethany Anne
for arriving neither too soon nor too late

List of Illustrations

Acknowledgements

For their help in the preparation of this book, I would like to thank the following people. First and foremost, Mr. L. J. Mitchell B.A. F.L.A., Director of Cultural Services, for his permission to use the Isle of Wight County Council's local history illustrations collection, without which this book would not exist. In addition, the following have given their help: Mr. and Mrs. Frank Basford, Mr. Roy Brinton, Mrs. Patricia Paterson, Mr. Don Vincent (who also drew the map which is reproduced as the frontispiece), the County Archaeological Centre, and Waterlines of Ryde. I am also grateful to the authors, both living and dead, of all the books I have used. Finally, I wish to thank the staff of the County Record Office and in particular Mrs. Dinah Slade for the coffee and the hints on typing.

Introduction

The Isle of Wight as we know it today only came into existence a mere 8,000 years ago. Before then the chalk ridge between the Needles and the Isle of Purbeck was continuous and the Solent was a river, flowing into the larger 'channel river' to the south. About 6,000 B.C. the chalk ridge was breached and the incoming sea created the coastlines of Hampshire, Dorset, Sussex and the Island, roughly as we would recognise them today.

The Island was inhabited from its earliest days, as archaeological evidence shows. There is an abundance of burial mounds, and implements such as stone axeheads have frequently been found. These early settlers were followed by the Romans, who built several villas on the Island, which they named *Vectis*. They were obviously a farming community but there do not appear to be any traces of fortifications. Carisbrooke Castle is frequently cited as a Roman fort but so far archaeological excavation has failed to find any traces of such early defences. Following the departure of the Romans, the Island was one of two areas to be settled by the Jutes as opposed to Angles or Saxons. (The other area was Kent.) In the seventh century they in turn were conquered by the Saxons, who had by now accepted Christianity. They brought it to the Island, which was one of the last places to be converted.

William the Conqueror was one of the first to realise the strategic importance of the Island with regard to the defence of the south coast. This was to be a recurring theme until the present century. William granted the Island to a kinsman, William FitzOsbern, but treason returned it to the Crown and it was later granted to the de Redvers family, who held it until the end of the 13th century.

The Hundred Years War in the 14th century brought a renewed threat of invasion and sporadic French raids. In one of the worst, in 1377, Yarmouth and Newport were severely damaged by fire and Newtown, until then a thriving borough, was almost totally destroyed. Further French invasion scares in the 16th century led to the building of a series of forts around the Solent area on the orders of Henry VIII. These included blockhouses at East and West Cowes, Yarmouth and St Helens on the Island and at Hurst and Calshot on the mainland.

The next major threat of invasion came in 1588 in the form of the Spanish Armada. It was assumed that the Spanish intended to take the Island and use it as a base from which to launch their attack on the rest of England. In the end the Spanish abandoned this plan but it was kept as an alternative to the actual plan of sailing to Holland to rendezvous with troops there. The Islanders knew many anxious moments once the fleet was sighted and it was only when it was well out of sight again that the militia was dismissed.

The final invasion scare that led to a large-scale building programme was in the middle of the 19th century. Again it was the French who were the potential invaders. Sweeping changes were recommended for the defence of Portsmouth, now an important naval dockyard. The Island was considered to be the first line of defence and many of the old fortifications were refurbished and new ones built, including those in the sea itself. The scare came to nothing and the forts have been nicknamed 'Palmerston's follies' after the Prime Minister at the time, Lord Palmerston.

The Island has always been an agricultural rather than an industrial area. Apart from the stone quarries and boatbuilding, there was little industry until the coming of shipbuilding and aircraft production in the 19th and 20th centuries. This dependence on agriculture explains why there were so few towns until recently. Most of the population was employed on the land and, with the exception of Newport as the market town, had no need of other centres of trade. Even 'towns' such as Brading and Yarmouth were little more than villages. Agriculture has suffered many vicissitudes over the centuries but on the Island the peak undoubtedly came in the late 18th century. The necessity of provisioning the Navy at Portsmouth and the lack of goods from elsewhere in Europe during the Napoleonic Wars led to an unprecedented rise in prosperity. Many farmhouses were rebuilt or refashioned at this time, which made the subsequent slump all the more noticeable.

The Napoleonic Wars were responsible for an upturn in another Island 'industry' – smuggling. High prices made illicit trade across the Channel worthwhile and smuggling took on an importance that it had probably not had since the privateers of the Elizabethan era. Sometimes the Island was used as a staging post for goods to the mainland – at other times the goods remained here. The isolated cliffs and chines made excellent hiding places although the Preventative men did occasionally make a good haul. However, it was not until the 1830s that they began to get the upper hand and the smuggling trade dwindled. By this time a third consequence of the Napoleonic Wars had begun to take effect. Europe was out of bounds but travel, particularly in search of the picturesque, was popular and the wealthy of England began to discover their own country. Areas such as the Lakeland had obvious attractions but the Island began to receive its share of visitors despite the difficulties of travel. The packet boat journey was long, difficult and uncomfortable as well as subject to adverse weather conditions and Island roads left much to be desired. However, once here, the tourists continued to come.

A growing population plus an ever-increasing demand for hotel accommodation led to the growth of many fishing villages into towns, particularly on the south coast. This explains why so many Island towns are Victorian creations. The advent of the steamship coupled with a railway building explosion completed the process. The Island tourist industry boomed as travel became cheaper and less restricted to the wealthy. The heyday may have been before World War One but it was probably only the appearance of the cheap package holiday that ended the British sea-side holiday. The continent was open again. The wheel had come full circle.

Newport and Carisbrooke

Newport was founded by Richard de Redvers, Lord of the Isle of Wight, sometime in the early 12th century. It was intended to be the port for the then capital of the Island, Carisbrooke. There had been settlement on the site earlier as Bronze and Iron Age remains have been found. However nothing permanent developed despite the construction of Roman villas in both Newport and Carisbrooke.

There is no mention of Newport in the Domesday Book although it would appear to have been an ideal site, being on the lowest fording point on the river. Therefore, it was not until the de Redvers family laid out their medieval borough that there was any large scale settlement. The plots or 'places' were let at a shilling a year per place (a quarter of an acre). In *c.*1190 Richard de Redvers III granted the town its first charter. Problems in the 14th century, including the Black Death in 1349 and the sacking of the town by the French in 1377, impeded the growth of the town until the 17th century.

Newport was the market town for the Island. The corn market was held in St Thomas Square and the cattle market in St James Square. The latter eventually moved to a site in South Street in 1928 after years of complaints about traffic problems, noise and the smell.

Although there are the remains of a Roman villa in Carisbrooke, there is no archaeological evidence of a Roman fortification on the site of the Castle. The name Carisbrooke probably derives from Wihtgarsburh – the town of Wihtgars and the Castle would appear to be a Saxon foundation. The Normans built on the Saxon fortifications and in the 13th century, Isabella de Fortibus put in hand a great deal of domestic building work and repair. She was a descendant of the de Redvers and was destined to be the last hereditary Lord of the Isle of Wight. Widowed in her twenties, she was the richest single woman in the kingdom. She never re-married and, having no heirs, she sold the Island to Edward I for £4,000 just before her death in 1293.

In the 17th century the Island and the Castle were destined to play an important role in English history. In 1647, Charles I escaped from Hampton Court and came to the Island. He was taken to Carisbrooke Castle by the Governor, Colonel Hammond. At first he appeared to be a guest but it became increasingly apparent that Charles was still a prisoner. He decided to treat with Parliament and after much coming and going Charles moved to Newport in September 1648. Negotiations for the Treaty of Newport ground on until Charles was removed from the Island at the end of November 1648.

Baldwin de Redvers granted part of Alvington Manor to the monks of Lyra in Normandy for a priory. The village grew up around the priory church, but in the 19th century began to merge with Newport as the populations of both expanded.

Newport is both the physical and commercial centre of the Island. The first railway arrived from Cowes in 1862 and Newport soon became the centre of a network of lines. In 1890, when the Island became a separate administrative county, Newport was the obvious choice as the centre of local government. It has always been a commercial rather than an industrial centre.

1. King James's Grammar School was founded in *c*.1613 by Sir Thomas Fleming and other local gentlemen, including Sir John Oglander and Sir Richard Worsley. The first master was Mr. Elgar. In 1886 there were 20 free scholars plus other day scholars and boarders. In 1648 Charles I stayed here while negotiating with the Parliamentary Commissioners.

2. The original church of St Thomas à Becket was founded c.1173. By the 1850s it was in a dilapidated and dangerous state and so it was rebuilt. Prince Albert laid the foundation stone on 24 August 1854 and the new church was consecrated in 1857. In the foreground is St Thomas Square where the corn market was held.

3. The Guildhall was designed by John Nash and built in 1814. Originally it was the market house and town hall. In 1887, a clock tower was added in the corner nearest the camera to commemorate Queen Victoria's golden jubilee.

4. Towngate Mill was one of seven mills in Newport. It was built in the 1830s as a corn mill. Between the 1880s and the early 1900s it was owned by the Weeks family.

5. Coppins Bridge, *c*.1870. This is the new bridge which was three times as wide as the bridge it replaced in 1828. Just to the right is the Reform Wharf where coal could be discharged for the poor without paying wharfage dues. Among the shops are a pork butcher, a mantua and dressmaker, a greengrocer and a boot and shoe dealer.

6. Shide crossing. The Sandown-Newport line was opened in 1875 and completed in 1879 with two bridges at the Newport end, including one at Coppins Bridge.

7. The Isle of Wight Central Railway was created in 1887 when the Cowes-Newport and the Ryde-Newport companies amalgamated. No. 12 engine was built in 1880 and came to the Island in 1903, having been bought from the London, Brighton and South Coast Railway at a cost of £725.

8. Newport Quay. Coal seems to be the major cargo coming into Newport and in the early 20th century there were certainly many coal storage depots in the area.

9. In 1885 the shopkeepers in St James's Street and elsewhere decorated their shops to celebrate the wedding of Queen Victoria's youngest daughter, Beatrice, to Prince Henry of Battenburg. The couple were married in Whippingham church on 23 July.

10. St James's Square. In 1897, Queen Victoria celebrated her diamond jubilee. On 24 July, the Mayor and Corporation presented an address. In the carriage with the Queen are Beatrice, her daughter Ena (behind the carriage lamp) and Princess Aribert of Anhalt (Marie Louise of Schleswig-Holstein). The band is of the 5th (Isle of Wight, Princess Beatrice's) Volunteer Battalion the Hampshire Regiment.

11. St James's Square, 1899. The cattle market began in 1532 and continued here until 1928. On the left is the Corn Exchange which was built in 1890 on the site of the *Hare and Hounds Inn*. In 1928 it was sold to Barclays Bank, which still occupies the site today.

12.   At four o'clock on 13 August 1903, Princess Beatrice, the Governor of the Isle of Wight, unveiled a memorial to her mother, Queen Victoria, in St James's Square. The monument was designed by Percy Stone, a noted local antiquarian. The 5th (Isle of Wight, Princess Beatrice's) Rifle Volunteers provided the guard of honour. In the stands are members of the Corporation and chief subscribers.

13. The first executive committee of the Lady Foresters of St Simeon's Lodge, Newport, formed in 1895.

14. In January 1906, the Liberal Sir Godfrey Baring ended 25 years of Conservative representation of the Island when he defeated Lt. Col. Hickman-Morgan by 1,561 votes. The results were announced at noon on 25 January at the Guildhall. In 1910, Sir Godfrey lost the seat to another Conservative, Douglas Hall, by 291 votes.

15. Albany Barracks were constructed in 1798. Originally known as Parkhurst Barracks, the name was changed as a compliment to the Duke of York and Albany (the brother of George IV), the Commander-in-Chief.

16. John Milne went to Tokyo in 1876 to become a professor of engineering. While there, he developed an interest in both earthquakes and the Japanese lifestyle. In 1881 he married Tone Horakawa. In 1893 he returned to England and set up a seismological laboratory at his Shide home. He died in 1913, having founded the modern science of seismology. This photograph is believed to show members of the committee of the British Seismological Association.

17. James Richard Wise ran this store at No. 86 Hunnyhill between 1895 and 1906. He also had a tobacconist's shop at No. 95.

18.   The gatehouse, Carisbrooke Castle. The castle is of Saxon origin, with Norman fortifications built on top. The lower parts of the drum towers were built *c*.1335 and the upper parts were added in 1470. The castle was kept in good repair until the 18th century.

19.   In the foreground are the ruins of the chapel of St Nicholas-in-Castro. There has been a chapel on the site since 1070. It has twice been rebuilt and demolished and in 1904 it was rebuilt again to commemorate the 250th anniversary of the execution of Charles I. In the centre is the Governor's residence, built between 1385 and 1397.

20.   The courtyard side of the gatehouse was built in the 13th century and extended in 1335. There are three consecutive portcullis grooves which show how it was enlarged. The gates themselves are original.

21. In the centre of this photograph is the millpond for Carisbrooke Mill (also variously known as Kent's Castle, or King's Mill). It probably dates from the 14th century and was working until 1939. In the background, on the left, is the cemetery, which was opened as a ten-acre site in 1858 and enlarged in 1894.

22. Carisbrooke village. In the foreground is the millpond for Priory Mill, lower down Lukely Brook. The millers there were frequently in dispute with Carisbrooke Mill, as the latter could withhold water. Priory Mill was bought by the Newport and Carisbrooke Water Company in 1848 and sold to the Borough of Newport in 1876.

23. The tower is that of St Mary's church, originally a priory church of Norman origin, founded by Baldwin de Redvers. It is possible that there was a previous foundation on the site. The priory itself was finally finished in 1414. The church tower is also 15th-century, probably built in the 1460s.

24. Carisbrooke High Street, c.1875.

25. The *Red Lion* is an older establishment than the *Castle Hotel*, although it only dates from the 1830s.

26.   The Priory was built in the 1860s for a group of Dominican sisters who came from Stoneyhurst in Lancashire. The Countess of Clare was the main benefactor as she donated £12,000, the greater part of the cost of construction. The foundation stone was laid on 8 August 1865 and the first mass was said on 13 December 1866, two days after the nuns arrived.

27.   This is probably a bus from the Isle of Wight Express Motor Omnibus Company, which was formed in 1905. There may have been a special excursion to the Castle as it is not on a direct route to anywhere. The Company did have a regular service through Carisbrooke.

East and West Cowes

East and West Cowes both grew out of large parishes that are now subsidiary to them. Whippingham, on the east bank of the Medina, is the older settlement as it dates from Saxon times. Nothing remains of the Saxon church of St Mildred as it was twice demolished and rebuilt in the 19th century. Northwood, on the west bank, was just that: the north wood of a then much larger Parkhurst Forest. The church here dates from the 12th century.

In the late 1530s two forts were built, one on either side of the estuary. That at East Cowes only survived a few years before being demolished and the exact site is unknown. The one at West Cowes still exists in a greatly modified form and since 1854 has been the home of the Royal Yacht Squadron, one of the most exclusive clubs in the world.

With such a fine natural harbour, sheltered from the prevailing south-westerly winds, two small towns soon grew up on the banks of the river. However, like most Island towns, their period of greatest growth came in the 19th century. In the early 1800s the fashionable pastime of sea-bathing reached West Cowes. At this time the southern shores of the Island, with their better beaches, were virtually inaccessible and it was not until the advent of the railways in the 1860s that Cowes lost its popularity as a bathing resort. By that time, however, yachting had arrived. In 1815 a group of gentlemen met in London and formed the Royal Yacht Club (now the Squadron). At first, their meeting place in the Solent area was the *Royal Medina Hotel* in East Cowes (now demolished) but later they moved to the *Gloster Hotel* (also demolished) and then to the Castle.

In 1845, the ultimate seal of approval was given to the area when Queen Victoria and Prince Albert purchased the Osborne estate outside East Cowes. From then on, the fashionable world flocked to the towns, especially when the Prince of Wales (Edward VII) became the leader of Society and also took a great interest in yachting.

Both towns also have another distinction. They comprise the only area of really heavy industry on the Island and this again dates from the 19th century. In 1801 the shipbuilding family of White came to West Cowes from Kent. They developed a shipyard on the banks of the river and rapidly became the largest employer in the area. They were particularly noted for their lifeboats and for the high-speed boats they built for the Navy. They helped to develop both torpedo boats and destroyers. Later they went on to make boilers and engines and even aircraft components. The story of aircraft construction, however, really belongs on the other side of the river. One hundred years after the arrival of White's, the firm of S.E. Saunders came to East Cowes. Their speciality was light high-speed boats. It was the techniques of this construction that led to pioneering work in flying boats.

At the outbreak of World War One both towns were at their peak as centres of industry and the fashionable world. The industry continued after the War but the golden age of the Edwardian era had gone.

28. East Cowes Castle was begun in 1798 by John Nash as his own residence. His friend and patron, the Prince Regent (later George IV), visited him there. Nash died in 1835 and after several changes in ownership, the castle became the property of Viscount Gort of the Vereker family.

29. Norris Castle was built in 1799 by James Wyatt (a rival of Nash) for Lord Henry Seymour. The Prince Regent visited it in 1819 and the Duchess of Kent and Princess (later Queen) Victoria in 1831. Between 1880 and 1903 it belonged to the Duke and Duchess of Bedford, and Kaiser Wilhelm II (Queen Victoria's eldest grandchild) was a frequent visitor.

30. The first St James's church was built to Nash's designs between 1831 and 1833. Princess Victoria laid the foundation stone during her visit in 1831. Only the tower now remains as the church was rebuilt in the 1860s and the chancel added in 1870. Nash is buried in the corner between the tower and the west aisle (hidden by the gatepost).

31.   A steam floating bridge was first introduced shortly after the Cowes Ferry Company took over the ferry rights from the Roberton family in 1859. The fare was 1d., later reduced to ½d., at which it remained until the 1950s. Special provision was made for lady passengers – 'a person shall not smoke tobacco in the ladies' cabins on the floating bridge'.

32. Bridge Square. The vehicles are presumably waiting for the floating bridge. The notice on the wall is advertising the *Royal Medina Hotel*, which was the original Island meeting place of the Royal Yacht Club (later Squadron) from 1815 until 1826.

33. Osborne House before the Durbar wing was added. Queen Victoria bought the Osborne estate from Lady Isabella Blachford in 1845 for £26,000. The original house was too small and so was rebuilt by Thomas Cubitt to designs by Prince Albert. The pavilion wing (left), containing the private apartments, was completed in 1846 and the main and household wings shortly after.

34.   In 1890 it was decided to build a new wing at Osborne (right) instead of entertaining large parties in a marquee on the lawn. On the ground floor is the Durbar Room, possibly designed by Lockwood Kipling (father of Rudyard). Electricity was installed in the house at this time.

35.   A review of the five battalions of the Volunteer Hampshire Regiment before Queen Victoria at Osborne House in August 1899. This regiment included the 5th (Isle of Wight, Princess Beatrice's) Battalion.

36. Osborne Cottage was built as an 'overflow' house on the site of Osborne Lodge. After Queen Victoria's death, Princess Beatrice took up residence here.

37. Trinity Wharf was the Royal Family's private landing stage.

38. Queen Victoria's funeral procession passing East Cowes Town Hall. The queen died at Osborne House on 22 January 1901. On 1 February the coffin was taken on a gun carriage down to Trinity Wharf, en route to Windsor. Following the coffin were Edward VII, his brother Prince Arthur, Duke of Connaught, and their nephew, Kaiser Wilhelm II.

39.   The coastguard cottages were built in 1881. In the early 20th century they were taken over by East Cowes Borough Council.

40.   In the centre of this photograph is the *Royal Medina Hotel*, the early meeting place of the Royal Yacht Squadron. In the 1920s it was demolished to make way for the expansion of S. E. Saunders. Samuel Saunders came to the Isle of Wight in 1901 and acquired the site on the left of this picture in 1906.

41. Whippingham Rectory. Nineteenth-century life here was described by Rowland Prothero, Lord Ernle, in his book *From Whippingham to Westminster*. His father was the rector at the time of the second rebuilding of the church.

42. St Mildred's church, Whippingham. There was a Saxon church on this site which was rebuilt by John Nash in 1804. Between 1854 and 1862, it was rebuilt again by Albert Jenkins Humbert to designs by Prince Albert. It was the parish church for Osborne, and Princess Beatrice was married here.

43. St Mary's church. The original West Cowes chapel was built in 1657 as a daughter chapel of Northwood. It is one of a few churches consecrated during the Protectorate. In 1816 it was enlarged when John Nash designed the tower as a mausoleum for the Ward family. In 1867 the entire church was rebuilt, apart from the tower.

44. Fountain Quay has long been the landing stage for boats from the mainland. Communication with the opposite shore has always been important and it was the improvements in transport, with regular steam-driven ferries replacing the unreliable packet boats, that led, in part, to the growth of the Island's popularity.

45. Holy Trinity Church is often known as the 'sailors' church' as it was consecrated as the 'church on Cowes foreshore for sailors and seafarers'. It was built in 1832 at a cost of £6,687. The money was donated by Mrs. Sarah Goodwin. In 1862 the church was enlarged and in 1910 the interior was refurbished.

46. H.M.S. *Teazer*, 1898. Laid down in 1894, launched in 1895 and completed in 1899, this ship was one of the first destroyers. White's won a contract to build three, at a cost of £39,113 each. Considered to be rather ugly, they were said to be the only unsightly destroyers that White's ever turned out. *Teazer* was broken up in 1912.

47. These baths, with their separate establishments for ladies and gentlemen, were opened in the 1870s. Unfortunately, the proprietors, the West Cowes Sea Bathing Company, only caught the end of the Cowes bathing boom. The Island's southern resorts became more accessible with the growth of railways and the baths closed about 20 years later.

48.   Bellevue House was built in the early 19th century and enlarged in the 1840s for the Ward family, who renamed it Northwood House. It was part of the Debourne estate, one of three great estates in the Cowes area. The family connections are reflected in local street names – Ward Avenue, Bellevue Road and Debourne Crescent.

49.   Egypt House was originally called Westcliff when owned by Sir Thomas Tancred and stands on the western edge of the town. It was later owned by the Ward family. The name Egypt has never been satisfactorily explained.

50.   Queens Road. As Cowes grew more popular so more and more villas were built, either as summer homes or as permanent residences for the likes of retired naval officers. Queens Road was developed in the 1850s and was popular with European royalty. Edward VII stayed at Staffa House (the second house from the left) when Prince of Wales.

51.   The Parade. The *Marine Hotel* is the older of the two hotels shown in this photograph, dating from the 1830s. The *Globe Hotel* was built in the late 1840s. Both were severely damaged in a freak whirlwind which hit Cowes on 28 September 1876. The Emperor Napoleon III of France stayed at the *Marine Hotel* after his exile in 1871.

52. West Cowes Castle was built in 1538-9, one of a series of defensive forts ordered by Henry VIII. In 1854, it became the home of the Royal Yacht Squadron, founded in 1815. The members first met in East Cowes, then at the *Gloster Hotel* on the Parade (just to the left of this picture).

53. Apart from ship- and boat-building, yachting was (and still is) the town's major industry. Cowes Week was one of a series of regattas taking the yacht crews from the east coast to Torbay. Members of the fashionable society built their own villas here or rented them and British and European royalty were frequently seen, especially in the heyday, just before World War One.

54. The Green, between the Royal Yacht Squadron and Queens Road, was presented to the town in 1863 by George Stephenson, son of the famous Robert. This was to mark the occasion of the wedding of the Prince of Wales (the future Edward VII) to Princess Alexandra of Denmark. It was and is a popular spot from which to view the yachting.

55. The pier was constructed in 1901 and named, somewhat inevitably, Victoria Pier, just as the Parade, opened in 1897, was known as Victoria Parade. The latter was refurbished in that year to commemorate the Queen's diamond jubilee. The pier was intended to attract business from the many pleasure steamers in the Solent.

56. Medina Road was always subject to flooding, particularly at high spring tides. This is the industrial area of Cowes as J. Samuel White's is at the end of the road.

57. Charles Wesley preached at Cowes in 1735 while delayed
en route to America with his brother John. At first the
Methodists shared a chapel on Sunhill with the
Congregationalists until they built their own chapel in Bath
Road in 1804. In 1880 another chapel was built in Newport
Road, the foundation stone being laid with great ceremony, as
can be seen in this photograph.

Church of S. Faith
West Cowes. I.W.

J STANDEN ADKINS
ARCHT

58. St Faith's church was built in Newport Road in 1909. Although this picture was published in 1911, this is not the church that was built.

Yarmouth, Freshwater and Totland

Yarmouth is one of the oldest towns on the Isle of Wight, dating from at least the tenth century. The first charter was granted in *c.*1135 by Baldwin de Redvers, son of Richard, the founder of Newport. In all there were to be seven charters, the last granted by James I in 1609. The town was burnt twice by the French. The first occasion was in 1377 when they also destroyed Newtown and severely damaged Newport. After they struck again in 1543 the Castle was begun. It was one of the Henrician forts, contemporary with those at East and West Cowes. Yarmouth had the right (along with Newtown and Newport) to send two members to Parliament. However, the population of the town was declining, perhaps falling to 240 in the 1850s and so, not surprisingly, the town lost this privilege under the terms of the Reform Act of 1832. After this, things began to look up. The first steamship service to Lymington began in the 1830s and in the 1840s a breakwater was built to improve the harbour. A tollbridge was opened across the river in 1860 and in 1876 the pier was opened. In 1889 the railway arrived from Newport but in 1890 the town lost its borough status and became a village; a position not changed until the 1970s. Freshwater and Totland are villages but to omit them would leave Yarmouth as a rather isolated representative of the western half of the Island as all the other towns are in the east. The area of Freshwater has been inhabited since prehistoric times as archaeological remains prove. The medieval parish was divided into five farms – Norton, Sutton, Easton, Weston and Middleton. Sutton is now better known as Freshwater Bay. The church at Freshwater is one of the oldest on the Island, possibly dating from the seventh century. The church of St Agnes at Freshwater Bay is a much more recent foundation, dating from 1908.

Both churches have connections with Freshwater's most famous resident, Alfred, Lord Tennyson. His wife, Emily, is buried at All Saints (the Poet Laureate himself merits a place in Westminster Abbey). There is also a stained glass window in the church based on a painting by G.F. Watts. The face of Sir Galahad is that of Ellen Terry, briefly married to Watts, while that of the angel is Lady Tennyson, wife of Hallam, Alfred's son. The church of St Agnes was built on land donated by Hallam and the name was chosen by his wife. She also donated the porch in memory of her mother.

Totland is very much a Victorian village. It was only created a separate parish in 1894, having become a fashionable place for summer residences. Previously, as with so many places in the Island in general and the West Wight in particular, it was the haunt of smugglers.

Alum Bay is particularly famous for its coloured sands, caused by the upending of various layers of clay and sand into vertical stripes. Alum was mined here in the 16th century and there was also a fine white sand, valuable for glassmaking, which was exported to Bristol and London. Alum Bay has another claim to fame. It was from the *Royal Needles Hotel* in 1897 that Marconi began his wireless experiments. At first he only sent his messages as far as Totland but later he managed a distance of 36 miles.

59. Yarmouth Harbour, with the town of Yarmouth in the background. On the left is the Castle, one of the Henrician forts, built between 1538 and 1547. On the right is the tower of St James's church. The present church was begun in 1614 and finished in 1626, and the tower was raised in 1831. The coastguard cottages in front were built in 1862.

60. The Mount was the largest house in Yarmouth. It was completed in 1809 by Mr. Udall, a local builder, for the Rector, Rev. George Burrand. It remained in the same family until it was demolished in 1967, Emma, Lady Burrand, having left it to her grand-daughter, Edith Dashwood, in 1897.

61. View from Yarmouth Pier. The pier was built in 1875-6 at a cost of £4,000. The loan took 50 years to pay off.

62. *Pier Hotel*. Better known as the *George*, the name was changed in 1897 but was changed back again in 1929.

63. Wreck of H.M.S. *Gladiator*, 24 April 1908. In bad weather off Yarmouth, *Gladiator* was rammed by the liner *St Paul*, a ship twice her size. After the *St Paul* pulled free, the *Gladiator* was driven ashore on Sconce Point. Twenty-six men drowned, trapped below decks. Salvaged and towed to Portsmouth, she was scrapped as she was obsolete.

64. The causeway at Freshwater was originally the mill dam for what was probably a tide mill. The church of All Saints was a Saxon foundation which underwent successive enlargements and alterations from the 12th century. Emily, Lady Tennyson, was buried here on 10 August 1896.

65. Freshwater windmill stood at School Green but was a ruin by 1860. There have been windmills in Freshwater since the 13th century although not necessarily on this site.

66.   Farringford, the home of Alfred, Lord Tennyson, from 1853 until his death in 1892.
Not much of the history of the house is known but it is possibly late 18th-century with
additions made in 1840.

67.   A shop was established here at Kingsbridge by T. H. Moody in 1723. Robert Lever
(standing in the doorway) took over in 1869. By 1879 he was also postmaster and, as the sign
over the door proclaims, ran the Freshwater Station Postal Telegraph Office.

68. *Star Inn*, Camp Road, *c.*1900.

69. This public house was built in the 1860s as part of the new village.

70. By the early 19th century a hamlet had grown at Freshwater Bay, although previously it had been too wild to support even a hardy fishing community. The *Albion Hotel* (left, on the shore) was one of the first buildings. *Lamberts*, afterwards the *Freshwater Bay Hotel* (on the cliff above the *Albion*), came later.

71. Built in 1908, St Agnes church, Freshwater Bay, stands on land donated by Hallam, Lord Tennyson. The stone came from a disused 17th-century farm on Hooke Hill. It is the only thatched church on the Island. The building was designed by I. Jones from a watercolour by the Rector, Rev. A. J. Robertson, of his ideal building.

72. On 4 November 1916 the *Carl* was driven over the chalk bar of the bay by a combination of high tides and strong winds. A passage was dynamited through the bar and the ship was refloated.

73.   Totland Bay Pier was built in 1870. There was once a direct ferry link with Lymington.

74.   *Totland Bay Hotel* was built in 1880 and owned by the same company that owned the pier.

75. Totland Bay became fashionable in the late 19th century when many summer residences were built there. In the foreground is the lifeboat shed, built in 1884 by the R.N.L.I. for a new lifeboat, the *Charles Luckhombe*. The first lifeboat, the *Little Dove*, was bought by Island Sunday School children. The station closed in 1924.

76. The *Alum Bay Hotel* was built in the 1860s and was renamed the *Royal Needles Hotel* some 20 years later. In the early hours of Sunday 20 February 1910 it was burnt down. There was no fire brigade in the area but, with a south-westerly gale blowing, they probably would not have been able to save much anyway.

77.   A group outing in a bus in the Freshwater area. This was a popular form of recreation.

78.   The iron pier at Alum Bay was built in 1889 to replace a previous wooden structure. It was a popular stopping place for pleasure steamers until World War One, owing to the unusual coloured sands.

79.   In the background of this photograph are the Needles. The present lighthouse was built in 1858 to replace one up on the cliff.

80. Lifeboats were stationed at Brook and Brighstone in the 1860s but the station at Atherfield was not established until 1890. The shed was 75 feet up the cliff and the boat was hauled up and down over sleepers by a powerful winch. The first boat was the *Catherine Swift*, named after a Chale woman who left the money in a legacy.

81. William Cotton (known as Rufus) came from a large local family, well known both as smugglers and lifeboatmen. He witnessed the sinking of the *Eurydice* in 1878 while returning from France with an illicit cargo. He was coxswain of the Atherfield lifeboat and six of his brothers were in the crew. He retired in 1906 when the *Gem* replaced the *Catherine Swift*.

Ventnor and Bonchurch

Bonchurch was the larger of the two places until the middle of the 19th century. In 1811, Rosa Hill inherited most of the land in the area from her father. In 1829, at the age of 24, she married the Rev. James White and ten years later they moved to Bonchurch from Wiltshire. Three years earlier they had obtained an Act of Parliament to revoke the restrictive conditions of Rosa's inheritance in order to develop the land. Many famous people were attracted here, including Alfred, Lord Tennyson, Charles Dickens and Algernon Swinburne, either as visitors or residents.

Ventnor consisted of a cluster of fishermen's cottages on the shore at Ventnor Cove until Sir James Clark, Queen Victoria's physician, wrote a treatise extolling the virtues of the climate there. Sheltered to the north by St Boniface Down, the highest point on the Island, Ventnor enjoys an extremely mild climate with a sunny southern aspect and fresh breezes from the English Channel. Owing to the publicity, Ventnor grew rapidly. In 1841, when Sir James's book was published, the population was about 900. By 1851 it was 2,569 and had doubled again by 1871. The hamlet grew into a village and then into a town. It was never planned as individuals simply bought or leased land in order to build whatever they wished.

Dr. Arthur Hill Hassell founded the Ventnor Hospital for Consumption, later to change its name to the Royal National Hospital for Consumption and Diseases of the Chest. The Royal Family took a great interest in it. Princess Louise laid the foundation stone for the second block (completed in 1869). Prince and Princess Henry of Battenburg opened the ninth block in 1887 and Princess Henry (Princess Beatrice) laid the foundation stone for the 11th and final block in 1897. Queen Victoria was Patron of the hospital and her youngest son; Prince Leopold, was president at the time of his death in 1884. The hospital consisted of 120 beds in 1886 and 156 by 1904. In 1878 a patient was asked to pay 10s. a week if possible. The site is now occupied by the Ventnor Botanical Gardens, the hospital having closed in 1968, 100 years after it was founded.

Other developments in Ventnor included the pier. One was first suggested in 1843 but nothing happened until 1861 when the Ventnor Pier and Harbour Company began work on two piers in order to provide a harbour. One pier was finished by April 1864 but it was destroyed by storms and sold off in 1867. In 1870 the Ventnor Pier and Esplanade Company made its attempt. The first section was opened on 5 August 1872 and the entire structure was completed in 1881. However, the pierhead was too big and, after storm damage, the company found itself unable to finance the necessary repairs. The Town Board bought the pier rights from them and decided to rebuild again in 1884. The third and final pier was begun in 1885 and opened in 1887.

Ventnor, like the other southern resorts, continued to develop and attract many visitors, particularly with the arrival of the railway from Ryde in 1866 and from Newport in 1900. Famous visitors included the Crown Prince and Princess of Prussia (Queen Victoria's eldest daughter) and, at the opposite end of the political spectrum, Karl Marx.

82. John Hamborough built Steephill Castle between 1833 and 1835 at a cost of £250,000 including furnishings and improvements to the estate. Unfortunately, Hamborough went blind and never saw the castle completed. In 1903 it became the property of John Morgan Richards, an American and the father of Pearl Craigie, alias John Oliver Hobbes, a well-known author of the time.

83. High Street. Ventnor grew rapidly in the mid-19th century and the occupants of the first building on the left undoubtedly helped that process. Sir Francis Pittis and Son, estate agents, were founded c.1780. Alfred Scott (opposite) was an ironmonger and next to the tea-rooms is the Capital and Counties Bank.

84. This photograph of the corner of Albert Street was taken in 1871. In the background is the Congregational chapel, built in 1853 and enlarged in 1872.

85. Founded by Dr. Arthur Hill Hassell (1817-94), the first block of the Ventnor Hospital for Consumption was completed in 1868. The foundation stone for the 11th and final block was laid by Princess Beatrice on 31 July 1897. Queen Victoria was the Patron and the name was later changed to the Royal National Hospital for Consumption and Diseases of the Chest.

86. The Cascade. This waterfall was a natural feature but when the Esplanade was built, it was 'tamed'.

87. Ventnor front, *c*.1871.

88. A similar view, *c*.1890. This was the third pier to be built at Ventnor. The first two (1861-67 and 1881-84) were damaged beyond repair by storms. This one was begun in 1885 and opened on 19 October 1887. It was 650 ft. long and 25 ft. wide. A pavilion was added in 1907 and electric lighting in 1908.

89.   Ventnor from the pier. The Western Esplanade was developed early in Ventnor's career as a holiday resort, built in 1848.

90.   The Council School in St Boniface Road was built in 1906 for 250 children but was not the first school in Ventnor. A National School was built in Albert Street in 1859, on land given by John Hamborough of Steephill Castle.

91. Ventnor High Street, 1907. This photograph is thought to be of a rehearsal for an anniversary parade to celebrate the relief of Mafeking on 17 May 1900 or perhaps Empire Day (24 May). In the front rank are the Isle of Wight Rifles and the band is that of the Hampshire Regiment, of which the Rifles were a part.

92. As part of the celebrations for the Coronation of King George V and Queen Mary on 22 June 1911, the 4th Hampshire (Howitzer) Battery fired a 21-gun salute from the western cliffs in Ventnor Park.

93. Bonchurch was originally larger than Ventnor. In 1811 Rosa Hill inherited most of the land in the area and she and her husband, Rev. James White, developed the village, having first obtained an Act of Parliament in 1836 to revoke the restrictive conditions of her will. Henry de Vere Stacpoole, a noted local author, donated the pond to the village.

94.   The church of St Boniface in Bonchurch was probably a Saxon foundation but this particular church was built after the Norman Conquest. Although only 48 ft. by 12 ft., it was not the smallest church on the Island. A new church was built in 1847-8 to accommodate the growing population.

95.   Old St Lawrence church was the smallest church on the Island, being only 30ft. by 11ft. and 11ft. 4½in. to the apex. Despite the addition of a chancel in 1842, it was still too small. In 1878 this new church was opened. It cost £4,000, which was raised by subscription, and was built to designs by Sir Giles Gilbert Scott.

Sandown and Shanklin

The twin resorts of Sandown and Shanklin tend to be considered as one since they lie side-by-side in Sandown Bay. However, they did not develop at the same rate or at the same time, although both benefited from the 19th-century tourism boom. The Manor of Shanklin was in existence at the time of Domesday but there does not seem to have been any sizeable community until around the 16th century. Even this date is difficult to determine as Shanklin, Brading, Bonchurch and St Lawrence tended to be grouped together for any surveys. Even as late as 1846 Shanklin was described as a 'small, scattery village' by Lord Jeffery.

In the early 19th century, travel to the Island itself was difficult enough and most visitors preferred to remain on the northern coast rather than proceed further over rough roads with numerous gates. However, a few intrepid souls ventured south, including John Keats, who came twice, in 1817 and 1819.

The railway from Ryde was opened on 23 August 1864 and the development of Shanklin took off. The population in 1861 was about 450. In 1871 it had increased dramatically to 2,081. The number of hotels also rose from 19 in 1861 to 43 ten years later. Shanklin was at its peak in the 1890s. The pier and lift were built and the resort was considered to be the queen of all the Island. However, it was essentially a summer place. Therefore, the *Royal Spa Hotel* tried to encourage winter visitors to visit the mineral springs during the late 19th century but none of the other amenities necessary for a spa town were forthcoming.

The first mention of Sandown appears to be in 1086 but as part of the large parish of Brading it was probably frequently overlooked as a separate entity. The building of a fort at Sandown brought attention to the place as it was considered to be a prime target for enemy landing with its broad, sloping beach. This proved only too true when the French landed in 1545 while building work was still in progress.

One hundred years later this fort had been eroded by the sea and so another was built by 1636. It might have been put to the test had the projected French invasion of 1777-8 ever come about, as the main landing area was to have been Sandown Bay. Fortunately the plan was abandoned and although Napoleon reconsidered it, nothing ever happened. In 1864 the second fort was dismantled and a new one built nearer to Yaverland as part of the defences of Spithead. Yaverland became a popular place for military camps and exercises. By this time Sandown was also beginning to grow in popularity as a tourist resort. In the same year the railway from Ryde to Shanklin was opened. This passed through Sandown and whereas in the 1850s the place still only consisted of a few cottages, development now began in earnest.

96. Shanklin old village was the original part of Shanklin before the Victorian growth. The *Crab Inn* is reputed to be 350 years old. The sign against the house on the right is for Thomas Johnson, a house agent who also ran the post office, a circulating library and a bookshop, in addition to hiring out pianos.

97. St Blasius church was a private chapel for the lords of Shanklin Manor before becoming a parish church. Built in the 12th century, it was restored and enlarged in the 1850s. The dedication to St Blasius seems to have been made around 1900 as before that it was the church of St John the Baptist.

98. Situated at the foot of Shanklin Chine, Fisherman's Cottage was built by a Mr. Colenutt in about 1817. He obtained the first licence for bathing machines here and later had warm and cold sea-water baths. The Chine is Shanklin's most famous natural feature and the path and steps were first cut c.1820 by Mr. Colenutt.

99. Built about halfway down the Chine, this is the original Honeymoon Cottage. It was later rebuilt in the cottage ornée style.

100. *Daish's Hotel* is situated between the old village and the Victorian town. It was built in 1833 by Jeremiah Rayner and sold in 1839 to Messrs. Cooper and Daish for £1,050.

101. The view from Shanklin Down, probably taken in the 1880s as the pier and lift have not yet been built. Development is rapid and the villas have spread inland. In the middle distance is St Saviour's, the church on the cliff. Designed by Thomas Hellyer of Ryde, it cost £3,500 and was consecrated in 1869. A new tower was built in 1885.

102. The making of Osborne Steps, sometime in the 1860s, close to the present lift site. The first villas have been built on and below the cliff and Shanklin's population explosion has begun.

103. The lift and East Cliff. Proposals for a lift were first made in the 1880s. Talks took place between Shanklin Lift Company and Francis White-Popham, the lord of the manor, in 1882 and 1888 but nothing happened. In 1890 agreement was reached and Sir George Newnes built the lift, which opened in 1892, for some £4,000.

104. Shanklin Esplanade from the pier. This is the original part of the Esplanade, built *c.*1840 and rebuilt in the 1880s.

105.   A view along the same part of the Esplanade, taken after 1892, as the lift has been built. Moorman's Bazaar and Post Office was one of the earliest gift shops. The Moorman family had bathing huts as well as the baths and the Bazaar.

106.   Shanklin Pier was finally built in 1891, the first proposals having been made as early as 1864. In 1888 a tender of £23,940 was accepted and the pier was completed three years later. The Pavilion was added in 1909 at a cost of nearly £4,000.

107.   Submarine A6 was on exercise in Sandown Bay on 31 July 1906 when she came too close inshore and grounded at half past ten in the morning. She was refloated on the high tide at three o'clock. It was good news for the longshoremen as everyone wanted a boat trip to view the spectacle.

108. Possibly a picture of a bus on route no. 2 of the Isle of Wight Express Omnibus Company which began services in 1905. The route was a circular one from Ryde through Seaview, St Helens, Bembridge, Sandown, Shanklin, Godshill, Rookley, Carisbrooke, Newport, Wootton Bridge, Binstead and back to Ryde.

109. Luccombe was a notorious haunt of smugglers, as was Shanklin Chine. There was apparently room to store 100 tubs of brandy in the area. The cottages on the shore were occupied by the Kemp and Button families.

110. Built *c.*1150 as a private chapel for the de Aula family, Yaverland church stands next to the manor house. In the middle of the 15th century it became a parish church but was always part of Brading parish. It was 'restored' in 1889.

111. Lake toll gate. There were never any turnpike trusts on the Isle of Wight but in 1813 the Highway Commissioners were formed and toll gates introduced. Tolls were not abolished until 1890, when the Isle of Wight County Council came into existence. The toll was 3d. per horse, 6d. a pair, with a ticket for the next toll gate.

112. Sandown front looking west towards Shanklin, *c*.1880. In the foreground is the coastguard station. In 1886 the chief boatman was William Arnold.

113. *Ocean Hotel, c.1914.* The oldest part of this hotel is the gabled section to the right. Originally called the *King's Head*, it is the oldest hotel in Sandown, dating from *c.*1850. In 1900 it was enlarged and renamed. In 1902, Percy Stone wrote 'Our only old hostelry, the *King's Head* has put on a more pretentious appearance and undergone a rechristening'.

114. The church of St John the Evangelist. The parish was constituted in 1881 and the church was consecrated in October that year. The designer was C. Luck of London and the church was notable for its height. From the floor to the internal ridge of the nave is 60 ft.

115. Christ Church, the first parish church for Sandown, was erected in 1845. Previously, Sandown was part of Brading parish. The church was enlarged in 1863 and again in 1874.

60543.

116. The sea wall and Esplanade were constructed in 1889. Guadeloupe Terrace, on the right, was built by the Wheelan family, who owned the land.

117.   Sandown Pier, *c*.1880. The pier was built in 1878 and owned by the Sandown Pier Company Ltd. Three hundred and sixty feet long, it cost £6,000 which was raised in £5 shares.

118.   Sandown Bay. In the middle distance is Sandown Fort which was begun in 1861 and completed in 1866 as part of the ring of defences for Portsmouth and Spithead.

119. The Arcade. The Kursaal was a dance hall.

120. Pierrots were a very popular form of entertainment at the Victorian seaside. In the background are two bathing machines belonging to the Duffs, who were bathing machine and boat proprietors from the 1870s until World War Two.

121.   Military camp at Yaverland.

122.   This was a popular place to hold a camp. For example, the 2nd Hampshire Artillery Volunteers came annually in July for at least three years in the early 1900s.

123.   This is possibly a picture of Boer War veterans receiving medals at Sandown. This was the first war in which the khaki uniform was used instead of the traditional red coat.

Brading, Bembridge and St Helens

Bembridge and St Helens are villages but as they are situated on either side of the entrance to the once enormous Brading Haven it seems appropriate to include them in this connection with Brading.

Brading originally lay at the head of a large, natural harbour and part of the quay can still be seen, down by the railway line. Silting was a problem and various schemes were put forward to build an embankment across the entrance and reclaim the land. Sir Hugh Myddleton was almost successful but his embankment, completed in 1622, was breached in 1630.

In 1864 the Ryde-Shanklin railway was opened. This passed through Brading and ten years later it was decided to extend the service with a line from Brading through St Helens to Bembridge. This necessitated an embankment across the harbour entrance. The Brading Harbour Improvement and Railway Company obtained the necessary Act of Parliament and, financed by the Liberator Building Society, began work. The embankment was completed by February 1880 but was soon breached. It was finally made safe and the railway opened on 27 May 1882. The Liberator Building Society later ran into financial difficulties and the company chairman, Jabez Spencer Balfour, served most of a subsequent prison sentence in Parkhurst.

The town of Brading was probably a Saxon settlement, although there was a Roman villa at nearby Morton. The present church dates from the 12th century but there was possibly an earlier one as records link the monk Wilfred with Brading when he converted the Island to Christianity in A.D. 686.

The largest landowners in the area were the Oglanders who reputedly came over with William the Conqueror. The most famous member of the family was Sir John (1585-1655) who built the present house. He was an ardent Royalist and was imprisoned twice during the Civil War for his loyalty to Charles I. Unfortunately he died before the restoration of Charles II.

On old maps, Bembridge is marked as Binbridge Isle as it was virtually surrounded by the sea with Brading Haven on one side and the marshes of Sandown on the other. The Normans founded a settlement at Wolverton with its chapel to St Urian but the French burnt it down in 1340. Bembridge remained a scattered fishing community until the early 19th century when it began to attract tourists and wealthy residents. The church was built in 1827 although the first religious establishment was a Bible Christian chapel, built in 1826. The first hotel was built in 1830 and Bembridge was on its way. Around 1080 a Cluniac priory was established at St Helens which survived until the suppression of alien foundations by Henry V in 1414. The priory church became the parish church but it was subsequently neglected until, by 1559, it was 'almost utterly decayed' according to a survey of that year. The sea was also encroaching and in the early 18th century it was decided to rebuild on a new site inland. Only the tower of the old church remains on the shore.

124.   Before reclamation, Brading Haven was a large, natural harbour. Two vessels can be seen at the quay (centre). The first attempt to reclaim the harbour was made by Hugh Myddleton in 1620. Finished in 1622, it was breached in 1630. The Liberator Building Society Group succeeded in its reclamation attempt in 1880 but not before a breach added £10,000 to a reported cost of £420,000.

125. St Mary's church was built *c*.1200, and restored and lengthened in 1865. The town hall was the meeting place of the bailiffs and burgesses until the 18th century when it became a school. The upper floor was rebuilt in 1875. The ground floor was a lock-up and the stocks and whipping post are still in the arcade, also an 18th-century addition.

126.   The house fronts in the High Street are mostly 19th century but the houses themselves are probably older. Some may date from the 16th century.

127.   The oldest house in Brading. Probably early 16th century, this building has been a rectory, a public house, a guildhall and a brewhouse. At the time the photograph was taken it was a shop. The bones of Louis de Rochefort, a French messenger who was murdered in 1646, were found here.

128.   Little Jane's Cottage. Between 1797 and 1805, the curate of Brading and Yaverland was the Rev. Legh Richmond. He wrote moral stories including one called 'The Young Cottager'. Jane Squibb died of consumption but her Christian faith sustained her to the end.

129.   Nunwell House was the home of the Oglander family. The present house was built at the time of Sir John, an ardent Royalist who entertained Charles I. The south-east front was rebuilt by Sukey, the wife of Sir William, in the late 18th century. John Nash wanted to demolish everything and rebuild but Maria, the wife of another Sir William, refused.

130. The *Pilot Boat Inn* dates from at least 1830 when Bembridge began to attract visitors. A guide book of the time states '... a spacious one [hotel] was built on a most desirable spot near the beach'.

131. Bembridge Station was built in 1877, even before the embankment from St Helens was completed. The railway opened on 27 May 1882. The *Royal Spithead Hotel* was built in that year and both were owned by the Brading Harbour Improvement and Railway Company. The hotel was sold in 1894 and the Isle of Wight Railway took over the line in 1898.

132.   The High Street in the early 1890s. In the early 1880s, the inn on the right changed its name from the *Commercial Inn* to the *Old Village Inn*. The proprietor was Charles Woodnutt from a prominent local family.

133.   The present St Helens church was built in 1831 and the chancel added in 1862. The old church was eroded by the sea and now only the tower remains.

134. Built in about 1780, St Helens tide mill was owned by the Way family for most of the 19th century. They also owned other large mills at various times. St Helens mill had a considerable seaborne trade.

135. Territorial Army Sports Day on St Helens Green, 26 August 1909. Organised by 'B' Company of the Territorials, many events were open to the Isle of Wight Rifles and any other member of the Territorial Army. Princess Henry of Battenburg (Princess Beatrice) presented the prizes in her capacity as Governor of the Island. She was accompanied by her sons, Leopold and Maurice.

Ryde

Until the late 18th century, Ryde consisted of two hamlets – Upper and Lower Ryde. The area was then developed by the Player family, the lords of the manor. In the late 1700s William Player laid out Union Street to join the two communities together. It later became the main shopping street. The first chapel had been built in Upper Ryde as early as 1719 by Thomas Player but was subsequently rebuilt by his grandson George in 1827. Genteel visitors were soon flocking to Ryde despite the hazards of the landing. Until the pier was built in 1814, passengers were landed as far inshore as possible and then carried piggy-back across the mud. Jane Player, William's widow, had obtained a private Act of Parliament in 1810 to enable her to grant building leases on the Player estate in order to exploit this new popularity. Expansion was so rapid that by 1829 the area was recognised as a town in the Ryde Improvement Act of that year. A further Act of 1854 extended the town and in 1868 Queen Victoria granted a charter, incorporating the Borough of Ryde. The population figures give some indication of the speed of Ryde's growth. In 1800 the figure was approximately 1,000. By 1831 it was 3,676. Thirty years later it was near to 10,000.

Two years before the granting of the charter, Ryde had obtained its own ecclesiastical parishes. Prior to that it had been part of the vast parish of Newchurch but under the provisions of the Newchurch Parish Act of 1866 two parishes, those of St Thomas and All Saints, were created. Owing to its proximity to Portsmouth, Ryde became an important point of arrival and departure. The pier was lengthened and improved several times and the first railway, from St John's Road to Shanklin, opened in 1864 and was extended to Ventnor in 1866. A line to Newport, linking up with that from Cowes, opened in 1875. Finally, a line was built to the end of the pier in 1880 although a tramway had been in existence since 1864. Improvements followed rapidly on each other. A hospital, a waterworks, a gas supply, a theatre and several more churches were all built for the convenience of inhabitants and tourists alike.

136.   Union Street, *c.*1900. The main shopping street in Ryde, it was laid out in the 1790s.

137.   Ryde Pier, *c.*1860. The first pier at Ryde was built in 1813-14 to enable visitors to land comfortably. Previously they had to take their chances on the mud. It was a wooden structure, 1,740 feet in length. In 1824 it was lengthened to 2,040 feet and in 1827 it was widened. In 1833 it was extended again to 2,250 feet.

138. Ryde Pier, *c.*1890. In 1864 a tramway was added to the pier to link up with the railway from
Shanklin. At first the trams were horse-drawn but, in 1886, the line was electrified. In 1877, a new pier
was built alongside the existing one to take a railway line, which was opened in 1880.

139.   Ryde Pier, *c.*1900. The Seagull Pavilion at the end of the pier was built in 1895.

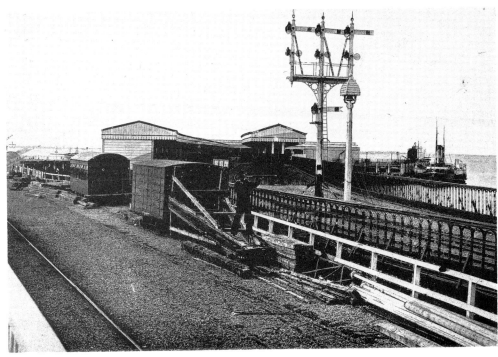

140. Ryde Pier Station. The paddle steamer is the *Victoria*. Built at a cost of £17,300, she was the first double-ended paddle steamer. She was in service between 1881 and 1899.

141. St Thomas's church. The original chapel was built in 1719 and paid for by Thomas Player, lord of the manor. It was a chapel-of-ease to Newchurch, the mother parish. In 1827, it was rebuilt by Thomas's grandson, George, at a cost of £3,500. In 1866 the parish of Ryde came into being and St Thomas's became the parish church.

142. St Michael and All Angels, Swanmore. A temporary church was erected here in 1857 as a gift from Mrs. Wray. Money for a permanent church was raised by subscription between 1858 and 1865. In all, £3,935 14s. 5d. was raised. Designed by Rev. William Grey, the foundation stone was laid at Easter 1861. Opened in April 1862, the church was consecrated in August 1863. In 1880 an organ was installed, bought from Torquay for £100.

143. The parish of All Saints was created under the Newchurch Parish Act, 1866. A temporary church was erected and building began on the permanent church in April 1869. The foundation stone was laid by Princess Christian of Schleswig-Holstein (Princess Helena) on 4 August 1869. Designed by Sir Giles Gilbert Scott, it was consecrated in 1872. The spire was completed in June 1882.

144.   Town Hall. Built in 1829-30, the ground floor and centre section were designed by James Sanderson. The first floor on the right was designed by Dashwood and built in the 1860s. There is no first floor on the left. A market was held on the ground floor but was closed in 1914 when the takings for the year amounted to 1s. 6d.

145.& 146.   Two views of Ryde Canoe Lake. This was completed in 1880 as part of the Esplanade. The plan was to extend the walk to Seaview but the residents there opposed the idea.

147.   The Isle of Wight Preparatory College was set up by a group of local gentlemen in 1879. The tuition fees for the boys, both day pupils and boarders, ranged from £18 to £30 a year. In 1905 the college was wound up for financial reasons. The house was sold to a group of Benedictine nuns and became St Cecilia's Abbey.

66302.

148.   The original part of Ryde Esplanade was built between 1855 and 1857 on 20 acres of reclaimed land at a cost of £5,000. This photograph was taken from *Ryde Pier Hotel* in 1913 and shows three forms of public transport, horse-drawn carriages, taxis and omnibuses.

149. The fire brigade was a voluntary body administered by a special committee of Ryde Corporation. This photograph was taken by Hugh R. Nichols who was in business between 1910 and World War Two.

150. Puckpool Battery was built between 1863 and 1865 as part of the defences of the eastern Solent. These guns were removed as part of the extensive alterations between 1898 and 1900.

151. Petty Officer John Ernest Humber died from blood poisoning following a bicycle accident. He was stationed at Osborne Naval College but was a Ryde man. The firing party (foreground) at his funeral on 26 March 1913 consisted of 40 men from H.M.S. *Victory*.